Hope

for the

Troubled Heart

Expository Reflections from Psalms 43, 56 and 30

Richard Caldwell

Published by:
Kress Biblical Resources
www.kressbiblical.com

Unless otherwise indicated, all scripture quotations are from the ESV®
Bible (The Holy Bible, English Standard Version®), copyright © 2001
by Crossway, a publishing ministry of Good News Publishers. Used by
permission. All rights reserved.

ISBN: 978-1-934952-56-6

Contents

4

Preface

Are you going through a difficult time—feeling like your world is falling apart? Do you wonder if God really hears your cries? Do you have pain so deep that you cannot fully express it? God offers His comfort in the Psalms. This little book contains studies of three psalms that are particularly good to look at in times of crisis—43, 56 and 30. These studies come to you with a prayer that they will aid you in your crisis. May the Lord, who inspired all the Bible, grant you comfort and encouragement through these Psalms, followed by joy when the crisis has passed.

The Cry from a Storm-Filled Heart

Psalm 43

First, for background ...

Psalm 42

To the choirmaster. A Maskil of the Sons of Korah.

[1] As a deer pants for flowing streams,
    so pants my soul for you, O God.
[2] My soul thirsts for God,
    for the living God.
When shall I come and appear before God?
[3] My tears have been my food
    day and night,
while they say to me all the day long,
    "Where is your God?"
[4] These things I remember,
    as I pour out my soul:
how I would go with the throng
    and lead them in procession to the house of
    God
with glad shouts and songs of praise
    a multitude keeping festival.

[5] Why are you cast down, O my soul,
    and why are you in turmoil within me?
Hope in God; for I shall again praise him,
    my salvation [6] and my God.

My soul is cast down within me;
    therefore I remember you
from the land of Jordan and of Hermon,
    from Mount Mizar.
[7] Deep calls to deep
    at the roar of your waterfalls;
all your breakers and your waves
    have gone over me.

8

[8] By day the LORD commands his steadfast love,
  and at night his song is with me,
  a prayer to the God of my life.
[9] I say to God, my rock:
  "Why have you forgotten me?
Why do I go mourning
  because of the oppression of the enemy?"
[10] As with a deadly wound in my bones,
  my adversaries taunt me,
while they say to me all the day long,
  "Where is your God?"

[11] Why are you cast down, O my soul,
  and why are you in turmoil within me?
Hope in God; for I shall again praise him,
  my salvation and my God.

Psalm 43

¹ Vindicate me, O God, and defend my cause
  against an ungodly people,
from the deceitful and unjust man
  deliver me!
² For you are the God in whom I take refuge;
  why have you rejected me?
Why do I go about mourning
  because of the oppression of the enemy?

³ Send out your light and your truth;
  let them lead me;
let them bring me to your holy hill
  and to your dwelling!
⁴ Then I will go to the altar of God,
  to God my exceeding joy,
and I will praise you with the lyre,
  O God, my God.

⁵ Why are you cast down, O my soul,
  and why are you in turmoil within me?
Hope in God; for I shall again praise him,
  my salvation and my God.

INTRODUCTION TO PSALM 43

We find in the 43rd Psalm **the cry of a storm-filled heart** that has the capacity to find its hope in God, and one that can be calmed by God. This is true of every believer. Sometimes our hearts are filled with troubles, but we have the capacity in God to know a peace, calm and joy that He imparts to us.

Our trials come in many shapes, sizes and forms. We face them in moments of crisis and in moments of relative peace, but always, we are the ones who are really on trial. You are on trial. I am on trial. Our faith is on trial.

James 1:2 *Count it all joy, my brothers, when you meet trials of various kinds, for you know that the testing of your faith produces steadfastness. And let steadfastness have its full effect, that you may be perfect and complete, lacking in nothing.*

In the midst of a trial, our true desires are being tested. What do you most want? That is what is put to the test when you and I go through difficult circumstances.

We're going to look carefully at Psalm 43, but to do that, we must also give some consideration to Psalm 42. There is evidence that these two psalms were meant to be read together. Psalm 43 serves as an epilogue to Psalm 42. Notice that there is no superscription that precedes the 43rd Psalm. Besides Psalm 43, Psalm 71 is the only other one in the Second Book of the Psalms (42-72) that does not have a superscription. So, it's as if the introduction to Psalm 42 also speaks for Psalm 43.

In addition to that, the refrain in verses 5 and 11 of Psalm 42 is repeated in Psalm 43:5. The words are identical:

Why are you cast down, O my soul, and why are you in tur-moil within me? Hope in God; for I shall again praise him, my salvation and my God.

Having two psalms devoted to the same general distress is a good reminder that some stresses are ongoing, not leaving quickly. We could say it's almost as if one psalm is not enough, since the theme continues. Not every situation that causes us grief or fear is quickly alleviated.

To say it another way, our God, in His sovereign and good plans, allows us to face situations that require us to persevere in thinking rightly. We pour out our hearts to God, not just for a moment, but for a season—sometimes for a very long season.

The fact that the historical situation that prompted these two psalms is left unspecified, is a reminder that what is poured out in them could apply to a host of situations. Many believers have found their heart condition in Psalms 42 and 43, even when what they were facing was very different from the circumstances of the psalmist. The troubles are similar, and the solution is the same, no matter what your circumstances are.

One commentator dealing with the question of what the exact circumstances were, writes this:

> Even though the life situation remains controversial, it is evident that the psalmist was isolated from worship at the Temple. He may have been a refugee, but it's more

12

likely that he had been exiled to Aram, Assyria, or Babylon, and was in the hands of taunting captors. [1]

Notice how the psalmist is taunted in Psalm 42 and oppressed in Psalm 43.

Psalm 42:3 *My tears have been my food day and night, while they say to me all the day long, "Where is your God?"*

Psalm 42:10 *As with a deadly wound in my bones, my adversaries taunt me, while they say to me all the day long, "Where is your God?"*

Psalm 43:2b *Why do I go about mourning because of the oppression of the enemy?*

Both psalms have a similar organization. They alternate between lament and hope, a sense of rejection and a longing for restoration. Where they are slightly different is that in Psalm 42 there is more emphasis on introspection, looking inside. Psalm 43 has more emphasis on invocation, looking up and making his requests known.

---

[1] Willem A. VanGemeren, "Psalms," in *The Expositor's Bible Commentary: Psalms (Revised Edition)*, ed. Tremper Longman III and David E. Garland, vol. 5 (Grand Rapids, MI: Zondervan, 2008), 380.

THE BELIEVER'S CRY TO GOD
(43:1-3)

The first thing we see in the 43rd Psalm is **the believer's cry to God**. This is the psalm of a godly man crying out to his Lord. As we think about practicing what we see in this psalm, remember that it assumes genuine godliness: our faith and love for God are genuine, and we desire to please Him. Psalm 43 is **the cry of a storm-filled heart** that has the capacity in God to experience hope, to be encouraged in God, and to know His peace.

Psalm 43:1 *Vindicate me, O God, and defend my cause against an ungodly people, from the deceitful and unjust man deliver me!* ^{2} *For you are the God in whom I take refuge; why have you rejected me? Why do I go about mourning because of the oppression of the enemy?* ^{3} *Send out your light and your truth; let them lead me; let them bring me to your holy hill and to your dwelling!*

Defense

He's pouring out his heart to God, and as he cries out to God, notice what he's asking for. First, he asks for **vindication**, or we could say, for **defense.** The two things are joined in verse 1. *Vindicate me, O God....* In other words, "Demonstrate that the taunts are untrue; that the way I'm being treated is mistreatment. Vindicate me and defend my cause." He's asking God to be both his judge and his defense attorney. The psalmist needs vindication because he's under attack. He's asking God to act as his judge, and therefore strive for him against an ungodly people.

Understand that this is NOT a claim to perfection. No genuinely godly person, who pleads with God regarding integrity and vindication, is making a claim to be guiltless. This IS, however, a claim concerning mistreatment. This IS a claim to a relationship with God, and to a relationship to righteousness, that his attackers do not share. There is a difference between imperfection and ungodliness. We all are sinners, some **godly**, some **ungodly**. Godly people sin, they confess their sins, and repent of them, and strive against them.

His attackers are ungodly and deceitful, with no concern about what is just. From the 42nd Psalm you get a sense of their viciousness and wickedness. Even in this 43rd Psalm he talks about "the oppression of the enemy" (vs.2).

Psalm 42:3 *My tears have been my food day and night, while they say to me all the day long, "Where is your God?"*

Psalm 42:9 *I say to God, my rock: "Why have you forgotten me? Why do I go mourning because of the oppression of the enemy?"* ^{10} *As with a deadly wound in my bones, my adversaries taunt me, while they say to me all the day long, "Where is your God?"*

He needs vindication because he's under attack. His enemies seek to harm him, and he looks to the very God that they mock. David looks to God as his defender, his deliverer and his refuge. What he's really asking for is deliverance: *from the deceitful and unjust man deliver me!* He's crying out for the Lord to rescue him from these people.

Do you remember that the Lord is your Defender? When you are truly mistreated, and are under attack, when you are the object of the mocking and the scorn of ungodly, deceitful, unjust people, do you remember that God is your refuge? Do you remember that you can cry out to Him, and He is able to vindicate and able to deliver? Is that enough to calm your heart? In the introduction we noted that this is the psalm of someone who does battle with discouragement, but he has the capacity in God to know hope. Do you look to God as your hope?

I love what Charles Spurgeon said.

> One such advocate as the Lord will more than suffice to answer a nation of brawling accusers. When people are ungodly no wonder that they are unjust: those who are not true to God himself cannot be expected to deal rightly with his people. Hating the King they will not love his subjects. Popular opinion weighs with many, but divine opinion is far more weighty with the gracious few. One good word from God outweighs ten thousand railing speeches of men."[2]

Spurgeon is saying that for many people, all that matters is what everybody thinks about them. But for those who really know the Lord, what matters most is what God knows is true of us. Can you rest in that? What a resting place it is that God knows the truth! If, in fact, we have a clear conscience, we're able to say with the psalmist, "Vindicate me."

Remembrance

Notice also, it's a cry for **remembrance.**

Verse 2: *For you are the God in whom I take refuge; why have you rejected me? Why do I go about mourning because of the oppression of the enemy?*

---

[2] C. H. Spurgeon, *The Treasury of David: Psalms 27-57*, vol. 2 (London; Edinburgh; New York: Marshall Brothers, n.d.), 292.

This is powerful. He's not just crying out for deliverance, but for **demonstrated nearness.** He wants God to intervene in a way that can be seen and known by the enemy. We could say it this way: God, will You show them Your love for me? Will you demonstrate Your nearness to me? Will You show them You care for me?

In the midst of the attack he gives voice to this sense of abandonment that he's feeling. He asks, *Why have you rejected me?* He must wonder, "Where has the deliverance been up to this point? Why are wicked people allowed to oppress me?" He feels forgotten. He describes his emotional state as one of mourning. He's sad, and he attributes this not only to the oppression, but to the sense of distance that he feels from God in the midst of it. "Where are You, Lord?"

When God's love and concern can't be felt, when it is a matter of sheer faith, and we don't feel it, then our circumstances can feel the most difficult.

Remember, we are called to be faithful in such circumstances. Our feelings are untrustworthy. We must lean on our knowledge of the truth we find in the Scriptures, and on the fact that God loves us.

Nearness

Besides being a cry for defense and remembrance, this cry is also one for **nearness.**

Verse 3: *Send out your light and your truth; let them lead me; let them bring me to your holy hill and to your dwelling!*

He's basically saying, "Lead me to Yourself," in the sense of leading me to the place of worship. He's longing for the holy hill of God, longing for the place where God has manifested His presence among men—"Would You lead me to Yourself?"

We can go through almost any hardship when we have a sense of God's nearness. No matter what it is, no matter how hard it is, no matter how heartbroken we are, when there is that sense of the presence of God, that nearness of the Lord, we can go through it. But when the only way you know God's nearness is by faith, when your feelings are not cooperating, when it feels as though God has rejected you and abandoned you, when you're crying out, "Remember me; draw near to me; show Your love for me;" those trials are the most difficult. But that's where we're called to be faithful. Remember that our feelings are untrustworthy. We must lean on our knowledge of what is true from the Scriptures. God's love for His children cannot be canceled.

This man is not just desiring more pleasant circumstances. His desire is for God. Note how the 42nd Psalm begins:

Psalm 42:1 *To the choirmaster. A Maskil of the Sons of Korah. As a deer pants for flowing streams, so pants my soul for you, O God.* ^{2} *My soul thirsts for God, for the living God. When shall I come and appear before God?*

Physical reality is sometimes used to represent spiritual reality. Is the Psalmist thinking in literal terms when he says, *Send out your light and your truth; let them lead me; let them bring me to your holy hill and to your dwelling!*? He has been taken away captive. Is he longing for a return to the Temple Mount, or is he expressing a desire for a kind of nearness that he associates with the Temple?

Derek Kidner explains this and gives examples:

This prayer of verse 3 is worded in such a way as to raise the question whether it looks forward to a necessarily literal homecoming or not. To be led home by God's light and truth could mean being brought back from exile by the one who displays these qualities, but it is a rather indirect way of saying it. It seems at least a possible meaning that given this light and truth, the psalmist knows he can enjoy even in exile the very blessings of God's holy hill and altar. The Psalms often speak of such spiritual equivalence of the outward means of worship: e.g. 50:13f.; 51:17; 141:2."[3]

Whether or not he's thinking in literal terms, the psalmist knows he needs knowledge and guidance to get there. He wants the nearness to God that he associates with the temple, a place of joyful worship. To arrive at the place of nearness to God, he needs light. He needs truth. He needs God to send forth what is necessary in order for him to draw near to God.

The fact that he speaks of light and truth indicates that he's asking God to answer this request in a way that transforms him and brings him nearer to God. The Lord is the source of light and of truth. The psalmist wants to meet with light and with truth. "God, would You work in a way that leads me to the place of joyful worship?" Isn't that what we need in our trials, for God to work in our hearts in such a way that His light and His truth bring us near to Him?

Be encouraged that you can draw near to God in your present circumstances. God can impart light and truth to your soul right where you are. He can help you without

---

[3] Derek Kidner, _Psalms 1–72: An Introduction and Commentary_, vol. 15, Tyndale Old Testament Commentaries (Downers Grove, IL: Inter-Varsity Press, 1973), 185.

relocating you. Far too often we think the problem is where we are, instead of realizing that oftentimes <u>where we are</u> is a tool of God used to expose <u>who we are</u>. We need to be developed. We need to grow and to mature, learning to rest in God. We want God to <u>change our circumstances</u>, but God is at work <u>changing us.</u>

THE PSALMIST'S COMMITMENT TO GOD
(43:4)

Not only does this 43rd Psalm express a request, but also a resolve, **a commitment made to worship God**.

Psalm 43:4 *Then I will go to the altar of God, to God my exceeding joy, and I will praise you with the lyre,*

He has contemplated what the fulfillment of his desires will mean. How will he respond if God grants what he is asking for? The psalmist has already **resolved** in his heart that his response will be **worship**. However, this is not like the prayer of unbelievers who bring requests to God and make promises in light of what they want, bargaining with God, so to speak. "God, if you will do this, then here's what I will do. If you will grant my request, I promise that I'll worship you. I'll be devoted to you. I'll serve you." No, this believer's prayer is very different in terms of its desires and its goals.

The kind of worship he envisions in verse 4 is actually the answer to his desires. It would mean God has answered his prayer to worship God at His altar. His requests are not self-centered, not temporally focused, but God-centered and would be fulfilled in worship. He longs for the mocking and mistreatment to stop. But through it all, he's looking to God as his refuge, his helper, the One in whom he glories even when it costs him to glory in God. His enemies obviously know in whom he trusts, and that's why they are mocking him for that trust.

He resolves to worship God. **He resolves to praise God** in the ways that the sons of Korah were set apart to do. He would give God songs of praise. *I will praise you with the lyre, O God, my God.*

Notice, then, what he says in association with these commitments. He will worship and praise the God who is **his** *exceeding joy* and who is **his** *God*. These requests reveal what he's already found in God. He has already known God as his exceeding joy. He has already known God as his God. His desires and his prayer reflect the fact that God is *already* his treasure, and he longs for the fulfillment of his desires, which are set on God.

I mentioned before that we are tested in the trials, and this is one of the great tests. Is *God* really the goal of our desires? Is *knowing God* and *finding our joy in God* the goal of our desires? "You are my exceeding joy." Do you know that reality, so when going through a trial, your longing is to walk in the joy that is found in God?

Is giving worship to God your life's aim? Is personal, singular, devotion to God your ambition? When God allows trials that strip away all sorts of things, so that what you're left with is nothing but God, do you feel a sense of loss? This is the test, isn't it? What do you really want? Not just what do you truly believe, but since this is wrapped up with our faith, do you really want Christlikeness? God uses trials to form that, to form a deeper knowledge of the Lord who has saved you. He uses trouble to deepen our well. Do you want purity and holiness? Isn't it true that trials often are a purifying influence in our lives? *What do you want?*

Is this your heart's attitude?—"God, if You'll deliver me, I'll respond with devotion. And when I do, it will represent the fulfillment of what I already long for. My soul pants for You. You are my *exceeding joy*. You are *my God*."

THE COUNSEL TO ONESELF
(43:5)

Earlier I mentioned the alternation between lament and hope, a sense of being rejected and a longing for restoration. Notice how the psalm ends.

Psalm 43:5 *Why are you cast down, O my soul, and why are you in turmoil within me? Hope in God; for I shall again praise him, my salvation and my God.*

The psalm finishes with something that is desperately important when we are tested. The psalmist is preaching to himself. If only we would preach as well to ourselves as we do to others! What do you say to yourself? The third thing to notice in this psalm is **the believer's counsel to himself.** We're good at preaching to others when they're going through a trial. We have all our answers ready to go. But when it's us, what goes on in our minds and hearts?

DO NOT BE DISCOURAGED

What he preaches to himself is simple. It actually shows that God is answering his prayer, sending the light and truth that he talked about earlier. Here's light. Here's truth. He preaches two things to himself: first, **don't be discouraged.** *Why are you cast down, O my soul, and why are you in turmoil within me?* I don't control the external storms, but why am I experiencing an internal one?

There is a sense in which the believer's discouragements are illogical. God is patient with us. He knows our frame and is compassionate toward our smallness. But when the storm is raging in our hearts, when we know an internal turmoil, when our souls are cast down, we need to learn to

23

ask WHY? When His people hurt, He cares. Christ is a High Priest who has compassion toward the believer.

So, God is patient with us, but the fact of the matter is, our discouragements don't really make sense, do they? We need to learn to ask why. Why am I discouraged? Why am I down? Why is there a storm going on in my heart? Why indeed, when the Almighty God of the universe has saved you, reconciled you to Himself, when He holds your life so securely in His hands that nobody can snatch you out, as Christ said? And the God who holds you in His hands is sovereign over *everything* and is good. He loves you, knows *everything*, and is able to do *anything* He wants to do. His arm is not so short that He can't save. He's not deaf, as if He can't hear you.

In an instant, in a moment, God could change your circumstances entirely. So, if you, in your circumstances, know that God is sovereign. He is good, you are His child, He loves you, and He's all-powerful and all-knowing. What do you have to be afraid of? This attitude of hopeless fear just doesn't make sense, does it?

He's not only *the* God. As the psalmist has already said, He is *my God*. He's *our* God. One of the greatest New Testament celebrations of that truth is in Romans 8. It has a celebration of God having taken hold of us, and that celebration contemplates the worst possible future realities— persecution and even martyrdom. And yet, it is full of joy. Read it with awe.

Romans 8:31 *What then shall we say to these things? If God is for us, who can be against us? [32] He who did not spare his own Son but gave him up for us all, how will he not also with him graciously give us all things? [33] Who shall bring any charge against God's elect? It is God who* *justifies.* [34]*Who is to condemn? Christ Jesus is the one who died—more than that, who was raised—who is at the right hand of God, who indeed is interceding for us.* [35]*Who shall separate us from the love of Christ? Shall tribulation, or distress, or persecution, or famine, or nakedness, or danger, or sword?* [36]*As it is written, "For your sake we are being killed all the day long; we are regarded as sheep to be slaughtered."* [37]*No, in all these things we are more than conquerors through him who loved us.* [38]*For I am sure that neither death nor life, nor angels nor rulers, nor things present nor things to come, nor powers,* [39]*nor height nor depth, nor anything else in all creation, will be able to separate us from the love of God in Christ Jesus our Lord.*

If this is true, then *Why*—oh, why—*are you cast down, O my soul? And why are you in turmoil within me?* Preach to yourself, believer. Preach to yourself. Don't be discouraged. No matter what is happening in your circumstances, **you belong to God!**

DO NOT DOUBT, BUT HOPE IN GOD

The second thing the psalmist preaches to himself is, **hope in God; don't doubt**.

Verse 5 *Hope in God; for I shall again praise him, my salvation and my God.*

He not only questions himself—He charges himself. He doesn't just counsel his own heart with truth. He commands it. *Hope in God....* I must tell myself, "Richard, hope in God and know that you have a future. I shall again praise Him, my salvation and my God."

Charles Spurgeon, commenting on that verse, said:

> *"For I shall yet praise him."* Times of complaint will
> soon end, and seasons of praise will begin. Come, my
> heart, look out of the window, borrow the telescopic
> glass, forecast a little, and sweeten thy chamber with
> sprigs of the sweet herb of hope. ... My God will clear
> the furrows from my brow, and the tear marks from my
> cheek; therefore will I lift up my head and smile in the
> face of the storm.[4]

Smile in the face of the storm because you know God.
Hope in God, not in changing circumstances. Don't hope in
an outcome you predetermined. Hope in God and look out
the window of your circumstances and know where that
hope ends. It ends in praise and in salvation.

So, to summarize, what do you do when you're in the
midst of this kind of storm? What does the psalmist do? You
pour out your heart to God. You process your circumstances
in the light of truth, asking God to send the light of truth.
You praise God as a matter of principle, and as an expression of your belief in the truth. You purpose in your heart to
take God's gracious dealings with you and turn them into
public praise. You practice what every believer needs to
practice when in the pit of discouragement. You **preach the
truth to yourself**, to your own heart. **Hope in God; know
that you have a future!**

---

[4] C. H. Spurgeon, *The Treasury of David: Psalms 27-57*, vol. 2 (London; Edinburgh; New York: Marshall Brothers, n.d.), 294.

After the Crisis

Psalm 56

Psalm 56

To the choirmaster: according to The Dove on Far-off Terebinths. A Miktam of David, when the Philistines seized him in Gath.

¹ Be gracious to me, O God, for man tramples on me;
all day long an attacker oppresses me;
² my enemies trample on me all day long,
for many attack me proudly.
³ When I am afraid,
I put my trust in you.
⁴ In God, whose word I praise,
in God I trust; I shall not be afraid.
What can flesh do to me?

⁵ All day long they injure my cause;
all their thoughts are against me for evil.
⁶ They stir up strife, they lurk;
they watch my steps,
as they have waited for my life.
⁷ For their crime will they escape?
In wrath cast down the peoples, O God!

⁸ You have kept count of my tossings;
put my tears in your bottle.
Are they not in your book?
⁹ Then my enemies will turn back
in the day when I call.
This I know, that God is for me.
¹⁰ In God, whose word I praise,
in the LORD, whose word I praise,
¹¹ in God I trust; I shall not be afraid.
What can man do to me?

¹² I must perform my vows to you, O God;
I will render thank offerings to you.
¹³ For you have delivered my soul from death,
yes, my feet from falling,
that I may walk before God
in the light of life.

INTRODUCTION TO PSALM 56:
SAVORING GOD'S WORD

You never want to go out to eat an expensive meal when you have a cold. To begin with, you just don't feel well, and you're probably not going to taste much of what you eat. You might as well just look at it, for though it may nourish you, there will be little pleasure in it. If you pay a lot of money for a meal, it's because you want to enjoy it. There's pleasure in it, and the pleasure is not just in the eating. It's in the tasting of it.

Many Christians read their Bibles as if they have a spiritual cold. They see its truths and recognize that those truths are profound. They know they should be profoundly affected by what is there and may even speak about those things with profound-sounding words, yet have experienced little glory in their hearts. Their knowledge is just intellectual. They've looked at it, and to some degree have digested it and gained nourishment, but have they really tasted it?

I don't want to be like that. Do you? I will put it to you as plainly as this: I want to feel, not just think. I want to savor, not just see. I want to taste that which I study in the Word of God.

I say "Amen" to two quotes by John Piper.

> The main aim of preaching is not the transfer of information, but an encounter with the living God. The people of God meet God in the anointed heralding of God's message in a way that cannot be duplicated by any other means. Preaching in a worship service is not a lecture in

a classroom. It is the echo of and the exultation over God speaking to us in His Word.[5]

There are always two parts to true worship. There is seeing God, and there is savoring God. You can't separate these. You must see Him to savor Him. And if you don't savor Him when you see Him, you insult Him. In true worship, there is always understanding with the mind, and there is always feeling in the heart. Understanding must always be the foundation of feeling, or all we have is baseless emotionalism. But understanding of God that doesn't give rise to feeling for God becomes mere intellectualism and deadness. This is why the Bible continually calls us to think and to consider and meditate on the one hand, and to rejoice and to fear and to mourn and to delight and to hope and to be glad on the other hand. Both are essential for worship. The reason the Word of God takes the form of preaching in worship is that true preaching is the kind of speech that consistently unites these two aspects of worship, both in the way that it is done, and in the aims that it has.[6]

I would say that what is true of preaching is true of our lives. I don't want to just think about God. I want to commune with God and adore Him. I want to feel my sorrows and to feel my celebrations. I want to sense that I'm living, and to sense that I'm on my way to death, which means I'm on my way to an immortal, everlasting existence in the presence of God. You can be sober-minded without being morbid.

I don't want life to go on around me while I'm oblivious to it. Many people are living like that. There are

---

[5] In the Foreword to Jason Meyer, *Preaching: A Biblical Theology* (Wheaton: Crossway Books, 2013), pp. 12-13.
[6] John Piper, *The Supremacy of God in Preaching*, Revised, Expanded Edition (Grand Rapids: Baker Books, 2015), p. 12.

monumental things going on daily in their lives and all around them, but they go through life with their faces in a television set, a mobile device, business reports, or something else. Days come and days go, and they've never really sensed the weightiness of what they're engaged in. I want to feel the weight of life, but not in a way that's outside of believing and trusting in the living God.

LOOKING AT DAVID'S HEART

I love the Psalms. This is the place in the Bible where I go when my affections (my desires and emotions) feel thin. If God never meant for us to feel, He would not have given us the Book of Psalms, because they're full of feeling. It runs all through them. There are heights; there are depths. There are sorrows; there are joys. There are questions; there are answers. There are doubts; there are convictions. But through it all is worship. All of this is in the Psalms because it all is experienced in the life of one who walks with God.

David was a man who walked with God. He was chosen for great things, which meant he would experience great tests. God never does great things with anyone whom He doesn't greatly test. You can't point me to one person on the pages of Scripture who was given some great thing to do, some great responsibility, some great role in the drama of redemption, who was not sorely tested. Every child of God has been given great privilege and therefore, great responsibility. Every child of God will be greatly tested.

David now tells us about the kind of communion that goes on in the life of a servant of God in the midst of a great and fearful test. The Psalm's title tells us that this Psalm arose out of an experience that David had when he was seized by the Philistines in Gath. Yet the Psalm is written in such a way that it clearly applies to all sorts of persecution, mistreatment, fear, and that which would fill our hearts with doubt. It shows us how to worship in the face of that which we feel threatens us, troubles us, frightens us, and makes us feel our great neediness before God.

It is so simple and straightforward, and in that way, so gracious. When we are hurting, we need a balm, not a puzzle. David puts it on a shelf where we don't have to reach so high to get hold of it. Hurting people are often in a weakened condition. They need precious truth ready to digest. That's what we have here. Just take it into your soul and taste it. Reflect upon your own situation and realize just how faithful God is; therefore, how confident you can be as a child of God.

A PLEA FOR
UNDESERVED HELP
(56:1-2)

We have David's testimony, one that was penned after he got to the other side of a crisis. His testimony lets us into his heart *in the midst of* the crisis. He walks us through it all the way to the other side. It is a testimony of trust. Scholars and commentators have divided its thoughts in several different ways. We'll walk through it in a simple way, seeing seven parts.

First, we see a plea for undeserved help, verses 1 and 2: *Be gracious to me, O God, for man tramples on me; all day long an attacker oppresses me; my enemies trample on me all day long, for many attack me proudly.*

The psalmist feels the pressure of **human opposition**. He doesn't have just one enemy, but multiple enemies (vs 2). David describes this enemy in terms of mankind being **vicious**, verse 1. *...For man tramples on me*. This points to the true nature of fallen mankind. Mankind is like a bloodthirsty monster. Those who pursue David are cruel, relentless, tireless, hateful. They seek his life. In verse 1, the word *trample* has the idea of panting after, like you're dogging someone's steps. His enemies are also **relentless**. He emphasizes this when twice he uses the words *all day— all day long an attacker oppresses me; my enemies trample on me all day long....*

The opposition is vicious, relentless and **full of arrogance**. They attack him, verse 2, and they do it with a proud heart.

What does David do? He looks to God for help. It's very instructive how he does it. He pleads with God in a way that **appeals to His mercy**. *Be gracious to me, O God.* He needs and wants help, but he doesn't describe that help as something he deserves. He describes it as something that would be a mercy to him. Our appeal to God when attacked by enemies, is not that we are faultless. If measured by the strict justice of God, we all deserve opposition. And even at those times when the opposition we are facing has been unleashed in some way by our own sins or our own foolishness, we ask God for mercy.

A CONFESSION OF COURAGEOUS TRUST
(56:3-4)

In the midst of David's plea for merciful help, noting the nature of the pressure that he's under, in verses 3 and 4, we see **a confession of courageous trust**. He says, *When I am afraid, I put my trust in you. In God, whose word I praise, in God I trust; I shall not be afraid. What can flesh do to me?*

This choice—to trust in God—is a **faith** choice. *I put my trust in you...in God I trust.* It is a **principled** choice. It's based on his principles and on his knowledge of the Lord. It is also a **timely** choice. *When* he is *afraid* (vs 3), right then, at the time of his fear, he makes the decision to trust God.

It's an **emphatic** choice to put his trust in God. He wants to be sure that in these situations we understand who is the source of his courage and the object of his trust, so he repeats it: *In God, whose word I praise, in God I trust....* He's saying, in effect, "My trust is not going to be in the arm of the flesh nor in my own abilities. It won't be in what the world would refer to as luck or the idea that things will just work out okay for me. No, my trust will be in God."

Not only is this choice to trust God principled and timely and emphatic, but it is also **transparent**. David acknowledges that he gets afraid. He says, *When I am afraid, I put my trust in you.* This very choice to trust God means putting fear away. In the middle of verse 4, he says, *I shall not be afraid.* David means he will choose trust in place of fear, putting his fear away by trusting in God.

David's choice to trust God is an **informed** choice, informed by the Word of the God. The God in whom he trusts is the God whose Word he praises. God's Word supplies the content of his faith, and he has learned that it is trustworthy, so his trust is Word-centered. The Word is the content of his trust. This is how he has come to trust in God.

This is not some begrudging resignation— "I guess I'm left with nothing else except to trust God." No, it's nothing like that, because he trusts the God whose word he praises. It is an **admiring** trust, not begrudging or resigned. He admires and truly trusts the God whose Word he praises.

Finally, it's a **contrastive** choice because he says at the end of verse 4, *What can flesh do to me?* He sees that there are two sides in this battle. His attitude is, "Man sets himself against me, but I'm looking to God as my Defender, and if God is for me, what can man do to me? What can mere flesh do me when my trust is in the Lord?" To say that man cannot harm him is a confession about the <u>ultimate</u> and about God's sovereignty. Men can do great harm in the <u>immediate</u>, but God is sovereign over our lives, and those who trust Him are ultimately safe in His hand. Nonetheless, this is real stress. This is real pressure that could really make someone afraid. David's trust is in the living, powerful God who made heaven and earth and rules over everything. Trust in man, or in God? In the end, there's no contest.

So, acknowledging his fear, he chooses the position of courage by placing his faith and trust in God. And he does it in an emphatic way. *In God, whose word I praise, in God I trust….*

Will you dare to do the same?

A DESCRIPTION OF UNRELENTING
OPPOSITION (56:5-6)

Next, in verses 5 and 6, David elaborates on this **opposition** that he's encountering. He wants us to feel the pressure that he's under by saying it goes on all day. This is the third time he's mentioned this. People are panting at his heels, pursuing his life. They are bloodthirsty. They attack and oppress him all day long. That's vivid enough, but he's not done. He tells us more specifically what he is facing: *All day long they injure my cause; all their thoughts are against me for evil. They stir up strife, they lurk; they watch my steps, as they have waited for my life.*

First, he says, they are **distorting my words**. That's what it means in verse 5 where it says, *All day long they injure my cause....* The idea is a distortion and twisting of his words. It is a very insecure feeling when someone is accusing you of something by a distortion of your motives, of your thoughts, of your words, of your actions. In some cases, the Lord must be your helper because from a human point of view there really is no way to defend yourself. Sometimes, between two people, it's one person's word against the other's. If the other person is attacking you by distorting the picture, distorting your words and your motives, how do you defend against that? It's either true or it's false, but only the two of you really know. David is experiencing this distortion of his words.

He also says they are **inventing ways to hurt me**: *...All their thoughts are against me for evil.* There's contemplation and planning going on. They're considering how to do evil to him. The NET BIBLE® translates this, *They make a habit of plotting my demise.*

David's enemies stir up strife against him. The idea is that **they attack him or stalk him**. They're not forthright in what they do. Instead, they use stealth— **they lurk, hide and lie in wait for him.** It's like they're spying on him, watching him closely for the purpose of killing him. *They watch my steps, as they have waited for my life.* This severe, unrelenting pressure, apart from faith in God, would fill your heart with fear, keep you up at night and not allow you any rest.

What is it that has you under psychological pressure and keeps you up at night? What is it that fills your heart with dread? What is it that troubles your soul? It may not be exactly what David was facing, but God hasn't changed. His trustworthiness hasn't changed, and His Word hasn't changed. What is expressed in this psalm is just as true for your situation as it was for David's.

So, he cries out to God for gracious help. He describes the pressure that he's under. He confesses a courageous confidence in God, and a very specific kind of confidence. It is faith in God whose Word he praises, so the content of his confidence is described in terms of God's revelation. And yet, he wants us to know just how heavy a weight this is. This is no light thing that he's facing, not at all. The distortion of his words, the invention of ways to hurt him, the attack upon his person, the stealth that is involved, the spying for the purpose of killing him, all day long—these weigh on him.

A CALL FOR DIVINE JUSTICE EXPRESSING TENDER CARE (56:7-8)

It is not wrong, when one is wrongfully opposed, to ask God to come to our defense. David is doing this in verses 7 and 8. Wicked people are attacking him. Notice David's **call for divine justice that will express God's tender care for him**. He says, *For their crime will they escape*? He wonders, "Lord, will they get away with this? Will this go unanswered?" Then he cries out to God for justice, saying, *In wrath cast down the peoples, O God!*

David is asking the Lord to intervene, to defend him, help him, save him, and deliver him. He's already noted in verse 1 that he doesn't think he's faultless. God's defense will be gracious and merciful. David is not faultless, but he is righteous. He's not faultless, but he really does love God; he serves Him and truly represents the cause of God.

David is not being attacked by godly people, but by wicked people. So, he's asking the Lord to defend one of His children. And he's not wrong to ask.

With the right kind of perspective and the right kind of heart, you can do the same. When you are wrongfully opposed, it is not wrong to ask God to come to your defense, asking God to oppose wickedness. It is not wrong to cry out to God for His holy, fatherly anger to rain down upon the one who would injure one of His children.

David ties this cry together with the knowledge of God's genuine care for him, because right after asking God to do this, in verse 8 he says, *You have kept count of my tossings; put my tears in your bottle. Are they not in your book?* In other words, "**God, you know every step that I've taken as I have been pursued.**" The New American Standard translates this as *my wanderings* instead of *my tossings*: *You have taken account of my wanderings*.

When you're under pressure in this kind of situation, it's sometimes hard even to remember where you've been and where you're going. You feel like you're losing your way. In the midst of such a situation, David says, *You have taken account of my wanderings.* The Lord has counted every one of his steps. If indeed the superscription reflects where this arose from, here is David fleeing from Saul, under intense pressure. He says, "You know where I've been in my running from him. God, **You've taken note of every tear that I've shed.** You have kept them in Your wineskin. You have recorded and **remembered every moment of grief, every moment of heartache.** Aren't they all in Your book?" Of course, they are.

In the midst of your pressured situation, do you really believe that God truly cares for you and takes note of your tossings or wanderings? Do you believe He really takes note of your tears and of your grief and heartache? Is this true in your case, child of God?

A CONFESSION OF CONFIDENT TRUST
(56:9-11)

David now returns to a confession of faith, but this time, you'll notice that he does it with a **strengthened confidence**. He is confident that God truly cares for him. David is confident of **God's favor**: *This I know, that God is for me*. He's confident in **God Himself**: *In God I trust*. And he's confident in **God's Word**: *In the LORD, whose word I praise, ... I trust*. This is the solid foundation for prayer.

Charles Spurgeon said,

> The machinery of prayer is not always visible, but it is most efficient. God inclines us to pray, we cry in anguish of heart, he hears, he acts, the enemy is turned back. What God is this who hearkens to the cry of his children, and in a moment delivers them from the mightiest adversaries![7]

This is what's wonderful about preaching to yourself—you can begin in one place and finish in another. You are afraid, but you remind yourself of those things you believe and know about God. When you faithfully preach the Word of God to yourself and remind yourself of who your God is, what He does and how He acts toward His children, you can begin with a courageous faith. You look into the face of <u>fear</u> and overcome it with an understanding of who He is and what He does, finishing with <u>no fear</u> because you know these things are true.

With the knowledge of God's care, notice David's strengthened confidence. He says in verse 9, *Then my*

---

[7] C. H. Spurgeon, *Psalms*, Crossway Classic Commentaries (Wheaton, IL: Crossway Books, 1993), 229–230.

enemies will turn back in the day when I call. This I know, that God is for me. In God, whose word I praise, in Yahweh, whose word I praise, in God I trust. He has said it twice, and now he says it a third time. "I trust in God. I trust in God. I trust in God whose word I praise."

This time he doesn't say, "and when I'm afraid I'll trust Him." He says, ***I shall not be afraid.*** He ends on the same note. What can man do to me? This is **a confession of confident trust**, confident in God's favor, love, and faithfulness, and he is confident in God's answer to prayer.

Are you confident that when you cry out to God for His help, He hears you, and He answers?

Though the Lord is for us, and though He does love us and care for us, and faithfully answers our prayers, His ways are still beyond us. Circumstances don't always turn out the way we thought they would, or the way we would have preferred, but that in no way lessens what David says here. That's how faith operates—when we know that all of this is true, even in the worst circumstances, and we are sure it's true.

We may feel the pain of human opposition, but in the end, our place with God is secure. And so, David's eyes of faith are turned in the direction of God's faithfulness, and he knows that when he calls, God will come to his defense (verse 9). He knows that God is for him. He will trust in God and not be afraid. He knows that God's sovereignty rules over everything, so men can't do a thing to him...nothing! **That's the place of peace**. That's what we must believe and confess.

A PROMISE OF GRATEFUL WORSHIP
(56:12-13A)

At the end of the psalm, David turns his mind and heart to **what lies beyond the crisis**. We've seen how he has communed with God in the midst of the crisis, but now, as his confidence in God is strengthened, what will he do on the other side of the crisis? His faith enables him to look past this trial to what is on the other side of it.

In verse 12, he reflects on vows and promises he's made. **He promises grateful worship.** "I must perform my vows to you, O God; I will render thank offerings to you. I will give You thanks." He promises what Hebrews 13:15 calls the sacrifice of praise, probably involving prescribed acts of worship, but also expressed in the words of song as he's doing in this psalm / song. It's a good reminder for us. Deliverance deserves remembrance. It deserves to be remembered. And protection deserves praise.

Have you remembered lately how much God has done for you in Jesus Christ? Have you taken note not only of the eternal deliverance that is explained in the Book of Hebrews, but have you really remembered lately how often the Lord has been your helper in this temporal world? How often He has rescued you? How He has protected you and provided for you? How many times when your steps were wavering, He has solidified your walk, and how many times He has come to your defense?

We should be a thankful people full of praise for who God is and all that He's done. When you remember what He's done in the past, it strengthens you in the present and when you look to the future. God's past faithfulness is a commentary on His future faithfulness. He doesn't forget you, nor does He change. He hasn't stopped loving you, and He doesn't lack any power. When He's cared for you in so many different ways in the days gone by, won't He care for you in the days to come?

THE PURPOSE FOR A DELIVERED LIFE
(56:12)

David promises praise and thanksgiving, but it is very important to note how he finishes. He understands that **this deliverance is not just for *moments* of praise and thanksgiving—it's a *lifetime* of praise.** Look at what he says in verse 13: *For you have delivered my soul from death, yes, my feet from falling, that I may walk before God in the light of life.*

God's deliverance of us imparts a purpose for us. **His deliverance means our devotion.** It's **not just an act of praise**; it's **a life of praise**. It's not **a momentary** song of thanksgiving or sacrifice of thanksgiving, but **a life** of thanksgiving and worship and praise and devotion. This is what deliverance requires of us. David says, "You've saved my life that I may walk before You in the light of life." Have you made the connection between your deliverance in a time of crisis and responding to such love and mercy with a lifetime of praise?

David's thought is, "In a world of unbelief, there's just darkness, but in this life of faith that You've taught me and introduced me into, there's nothing but light. You've saved me to walk in that." Have you realized that? Have you seen that you've been delivered to be devoted to a lifetime of worship?

Here is how Charles Spurgeon described David's attitude in this Psalm:

> Walking at liberty in holy service, in sacred communion, in
> constant progress and holiness, enjoying the smile of
> heaven, this I seek after. Here is the loftiest reach of a good
> person's ambition, to dwell with God, to walk in

righteousness before Him, to rejoice in His presence, and in the light and glory which it yields. Thus, in this short psalm we have climbed from the ravenous jaws of the enemy into the light of Jehovah's presence, a path which only faith can tread."[8]

Understand that **we're not just to <u>see</u> these things, but to <u>savor</u> these things.** Seeing God and not savoring God, insults God. We don't simply acknowledge God's grace to us; we <u>respond</u> to it. And what is our response? We don't fear; we <u>trust</u>. We don't fret; we <u>rest</u>. We don't doubt; we <u>believe</u>. We don't respond to such mercy with a wasteful life, but with a <u>worshipping</u> life. We confess that <u>He is our life</u>, and we can trust Him, not because we're good, but because He is good.

If you are still in the midst of the storm, pray this psalm as your own. Preach the truth to yourself. Remember God's faithfulness and His past mercies. Look forward to the day when the storm will have ended. He **will** see you through. He **will** be faithful. He **will** be enough. By faith, look ahead and *walk* before Him always, in His presence, guided by His life-giving light.

---

[8] C. H. Spurgeon, *Psalms*, Crossway Classic Commentaries (Wheaton, IL: Crossway Books, 1993), 231.

Joy Comes in the Morning

Psalm 30

Psalm 30

A Psalm of David. A song at the dedication of the temple.

[1] I will extol you, O LORD, for you have drawn me up
　　and have not let my foes rejoice over me.
[2] O LORD my God, I cried to you for help,
　　and you have healed me.
[3] O LORD, you have brought up my soul from Sheol;
　　you restored me to life from among those
　　who go down to the pit.

[4] Sing praises to the LORD, O you his saints,
　　and give thanks to his holy name.
[5] For his anger is but for a moment,
　　and his favor is for a lifetime.
Weeping may tarry for the night,
　　but joy comes with the morning.

[6] As for me, I said in my prosperity,
　　"I shall never be moved."
[7] By your favor, O LORD,
　　you made my mountain stand strong;
you hid your face;
　　I was dismayed.

[8] To you, O LORD, I cry,
　　and to the Lord I plead for mercy:
[9] "What profit is there in my death,
　　if I go down to the pit?
Will the dust praise you?
　　Will it tell of your faithfulness?
[10] Hear, O LORD, and be merciful to me!
　　O LORD, be my helper!"

[11] You have turned for me my mourning into dancing;
> you have loosed my sackcloth
> and clothed me with gladness,

[12] that my glory may sing your praise and not be silent.
> O LORD my God, I will give thanks to you
> forever!

INTRODUCTION TO PSALM 30

The theme of Psalm 30 is clear and unmistakable. **It begins with thanksgiving and ends with thanksgiving**. David writes in verse 1, *I will extol you, O LORD,* meaning, I will lift you up high. "I will give praise to you," is what he's saying. He finishes in verse 12, *O LORD my God, I will give thanks to you forever!* "I will do this." This is a Psalm of personal thanksgiving.

But, as David is quick to point out, this is not just his story. In verse 4, he says, *Sing praises to the LORD, O you his saints, and give thanks to his holy name.* He calls upon us to join him, making this our story as well as David's. It is the story of every believer.

James Montgomery Boice, in his commentary on this 30th Psalm, made an interesting point. He said, "Thanksgiving psalms are usually expressions of praise to God for having heard a lament."[9] This is because these thanksgiving psalms often arise out of lamentable circumstances. At the time a believer is lamenting, there is sadness, sorrow, fear, concern, danger, crying for help and for mercy. God hears his prayer, and he experiences God's help, which results in praise. This is a good reminder, even as this psalm will teach us, that <u>whatever our sorrows and hardships are, if we are God's children, there is joy coming in the morning</u>. This is a 100% certainty, even if that joy is delayed for a lifetime. But it rarely waits for a lifetime. We meet with God's delivering mercies many times throughout our lives.

---

[9]James Montgomery Boice, *Psalms 1–41*, vol. 6 of Boice Expositional Commentary. Accordance electronic ed. (Grand Rapids: Baker Books, 1994), 261.

Do you realize that these times of sorrow and hardship are God-given opportunities to see our God put Himself on display in our lives? They are the backdrop against which we see the brightness of His kind dealings with us. As we'll be reminded in these verses, our sorrows are like an island in a vast sea of God's love toward us. Sometimes, those challenges feel like they'll last forever, but really, if you examine them in light of the whole of your life, you'll see they represent a very small portion of it.

As we walk with God, His pleasant dealings with us far exceed the times that test us. They are good, kind, and fill our hearts with joy. And even times of sorrows become the launching point for recognizing how good God is to us.

This particular psalm of thanksgiving celebrates God's mercy to David when he was delivered from some great sickness. It is clear that David was sick enough to die, yet God raised him up, and for that, David is now giving thanks. We don't know all the details, but he'll take us down into the depths of at least a partial description of what he was going through, and we'll be able to identify with God's mercies to him.

David calls upon the saints to join him, because his experience is only one example of that which is the common experience of God's people. We all encounter God's mercies in life, so we all should give God the praise He deserves.

The one striking literary feature of this psalm is that it is full of contrasts. When these contrasts are viewed as two sides of a ledger, what emerges is just how thankful we should be.

In verse 1, there are two contrasts:

- Being lifted up / if God had let him go down into the pit
- God helping him / foes ready to delight over his demise

Verse 5 has four contrasts:

- God's anger / God's favor
- A moment / a lifetime
- Weeping / joy
- The night / morning

Verse 11 has two:

- Mourning / dancing
- Sackcloth / clothed in gladness

PERSONAL THANKS
(30:1-3)

The series of contrasts throughout this psalm all place emphasis on God's goodness to us. How thankful we should be! This psalm has been organized several different ways by commentators, but we're going to study it under four headings. First, in verses 1-3, we see **personal thanks**.

Psalm 30:1 *I will extol you, O LORD, for you have drawn me up and have not let my foes rejoice over me. ² O LORD my God, I cried to you for help, and you have healed me. ³ O LORD, you have brought up my soul from Sheol; you restored me to life from among those who go down to the pit.*

In verse 1 he begins with a declaration of his intention to extol the Lord, his God, the true God. "I will do this," he says, "I will exalt him. I will lift Him up high," which is simply to say, "I will acknowledge the truth of the majesty of God." David's experiences put God's majesty and greatness on display for his own mind and heart. Now he desires to proclaim this through song.

What motivates David on this occasion is **a great deliverance**. David was *drawn up* by the Lord. It is a word that was used of drawing water, as you would draw water out of a well. And if you ask from where God had drawn him up, he answers the question in verse 3. *O LORD, you have brought up my soul from Sheol; you restored me to life.* He had fallen down to the very doorstep of the grave. As people might say, "he had one foot in the grave." I mentioned earlier that David seems to have been suffering from some illness. He was near to being among those who go down to the pit, that is the place of death, but he's been restored to life.

55

But what he wishes to emphasize is not only the deliverance, but that <u>God personally is his Deliverer</u>. He is extolling <u>the Lord</u>. It is <u>the Lord</u> who has drawn him up. It is <u>the Lord</u> who has not allowed *his foes to rejoice* over him. David has enemies, and these enemies were ready to dance on his grave. His death would have been the cause for their personal celebration, but the Lord has not allowed that. By rescuing David, He has not allowed his foes to rejoice over his demise.

David had *cried* out, verse 2, to the Lord *for* **help**. And it is the Lord who has *healed* him, and the Lord who has *brought* him *up from Sheol*. It is the Lord who has *restored life* to him and <u>delivered him</u> *from those* who go *down to the pit*. This is personal. It's not just about deliverance. We sometimes rejoice in our deliverances, but do we rejoice in the Deliverer as David did?

James Montgomery Boice had a good note on this.

Do we adequately think of sickness and recovery in these terms? Generally speaking, we do not, though as Christians we do tend to think of God and call to him when we are actually sick. We live in a scientific age, which has had the bad effect of removing us from a sense of God's presence and intervention in our lives. It makes us substitute secondary causes for the first Cause. We speak of "the miracles of modern medicine" much more easily than we speak of God's miracles or miraculous intervention. But strictly speaking, as thankful as we should be for medical knowledge, skills, personnel, and resources, medicine is no "miracle." It is a technology. The "miracle" even in contemporary medical healing is God's. So when you are sick, pray. Ask God for healing. And when you are well again, remember that it is God who has healed you, and thank him for it, as the psalmist does."[10]

Obviously, Boice is not arguing that we would forsake the means that God would use to make us well, but that we would not praise the means instead of the one who actually grants the wellness.

---

[10]James Montgomery Boice, *Psalms 1–41*, vol. 6 of Boice Expositional Commentary. Accordance electronic ed. (Grand Rapids: Baker Books, 1994), 262-263.

PRINCIPLED THANKS
(30:4-5)

In the previous section, we saw that David's thankfulness is personal, but secondly, it is **principled thanks**. In verses 4 and 5, David writes:

Psalm 30:4 *Sing praises to the LORD, O you his saints, and give thanks to his holy name. ⁵ For his anger is but for a moment, and his favor is for a lifetime. Weeping may tarry for the night, but joy comes with the morning.*

David does something here that we must not miss, nor forget. He's able to extract a principle from his own set of circumstances to see a bigger picture, that **God is gracious, kind and full of mercy.** His own life experiences simply reflect this truth about the person of God Himself. He calls upon everyone who hears and reads this psalm to join with him in giving praise to the Lord.

OUR DECLARATION

We have reason to extol the name of God just as David does. **He calls upon us to make his declaration** (vs. 1) **OUR declaration** (vs.4). *O you His saints, ... give thanks to His holy name.* So, he's basically saying, "I will give thanks, O Lord, to You. Now you, saints, join with me in this."

OUR DELIVERANCE

Our motivation for praising God is the same as David's. We too, have been delivered. All the people of God have experienced **a great deliverance**. This <u>deliverance results in the favor of God</u> and in an ultimate outcome that is never in doubt.

We have been delivered from eternal condemnation. By punishing Jesus for our sins, God answered His own justice. We were on the doorstop of the grave, in danger of going down into the pit, not just physically, but in an everlasting sense. The Lord has had **mercy** upon us, providing redemption through Christ, so we could become His saints, His holy ones, a people set apart unto Himself.

We not only see God's mercy in salvation, but just as David did, we see it in this temporal life, on our way to our final destination, the heavenly city. We see multiple deliverances in our lives during our lifetime, and the Lord is worthy of praise and thanks for this. Every child of God has great reason to give thanks to His holy name.

GOD'S ANGER AND GOD'S FAVOR

God's love for His children is demonstrated by His dealings with them, even when for a time those dealings aren't immediately apparent to us. We experience both God's *anger* and His *favor*. The *anger* of which he speaks in verse 5, is the disciplining hand of a loving father. The *weeping* is the sorrow that we experience in those times of discipline, but *joy* always *comes in the morning*. This is the pattern experienced by God's children. As God's child you can always know with 100% certainty that joy is on its way. Even if weeping were to last for a lifetime, that is just a moment when compared to eternity. Even if the hardship never lifts throughout your life, taking you to the grave in terms of your physical nature, the moment you open your eyes and see the face of your Savior, your sufferings on this earth will be as nothing in light of your future glory. *Weeping* is just for a short time, but *joy comes in the morning*, every single time, for the saints of God. Praise God that most of our sorrows don't last a lifetime, but only for a season. And, in fact, if you were to compare the time that we spend in the anger of God to the time we spend in the favor of God, the anger of God is but for a moment.

What does he mean here by *anger* and *favor*? David is describing how the Lord deals with us in His love from the vantage point of how we perceive it. Notice that he does not try to separate God's hand from our times of testing. The Lord disciplines His children, and sometimes it's corrective in nature. And so, when we are under the disciplining hand of our Father, especially when it's corrective in nature, it feels like anger, and indeed, it is a fatherly kind of anger—a holy, loving kind of anger. Make no mistake about it, God's motive toward His children in the midst of a test is completely different from that of our spiritual enemy. We meet with tests and temptations in the same events. What the enemy means for evil, God means for our good, but in that same event may be great sorrow. Weeping does not describe a stoic reaction. The pain is real.

Hebrews 12:11 *For the moment all discipline seems painful rather than pleasant, but later it yields the peaceful fruit of righteousness to those who have been trained by it.*

When we are not in a place of discipline, and it seems like the sun is shining and everything is well, that's God's favor. If you compared the amount of time we spend experiencing the anger of the Lord, with the amount of time we spend experiencing the Lord's favor, *anger is but for a moment.* And we must remember that even the anger of God in this fatherly relationship with His children, is just His love toward them.

So, in these verses David is extolling God for saving him, healing him, restoring his life, and for God's great mercy, but is also focusing our attention on the **Deliverer Himself**, and how He deals with His people.

The Lord's discipline of His sons is described in Hebrews 12:6 using the strong word "scourge" (NASB) or "chastise" (ESV) <u>as an expression of His fatherly love</u> for us. If we think about how we love and deal with our children, that is an imperfect reminder of what it means for a child of God to experience the anger of God. Do we realize that there can be no love without anger? Think about this in the human realm for a moment, although it's an imperfect illustration, because we are imperfect disciplinarians. A parent who never gets upset with their offspring over things that would destroy that child, is a parent that doesn't really love that child.

Heb. 12:6 *For the Lord disciplines the one he loves, and chastises every son whom he receives."*

For example, suppose I have a gated swimming pool in my backyard, and have instructed my 7-year-old son never to enter that gate without someone outside to watch him. Later, if I find him swimming by himself in the deep end, I'm going to be angry. He would not misunderstand that anger, would he? The only reason a father would be angry in that situation is because he loves his son. He's watching over him and caring about his wellbeing. No one would misunderstand this father's anger if the pattern of the father's relationship with the son is one of love, and the son has violated his father's will by swimming in that pool without supervision. This is a father's loving anger.

So, when a child of God begins to walk in things that violate the will of God—a will that is good, safe, and the source of our joy, our blessing, and our fulfillment—God now brings His disciplining hand down upon you. That kind of anger is nothing but love. It seems that the psalmist may be describing this anger in the terms of our perceptions: what we perceive in our feelings and circumstances to be the frowning countenances of God. But just when it seems dark, heavy and hard, even that is for our good, if we could see our circumstances from the vantage point of heaven. And yet, even this loving anger is not the <u>continual</u> experience of God's child, but <u>momentary</u>. We know this in seasons of trial, and sometimes these seasons seem to last forever, but they don't. In fact, they are just moments in a lifetime of favor.

As I said, though, sometimes it doesn't feel momentary. For example, those of us who live in the Houston area through a time of heavy rainfall day after day, with flooding, may say to ourselves, "It's raining every day; will it ever stop raining?" But if, for a moment, we stop thinking about how it seems, and we really trace how many hours of sunshine we experience in a year, versus the hours when it's raining, we would see that the thunderstorms are something we experience <u>occasionally</u>, not <u>continually</u>.

I want to emphasize that this is only true if you really know the Lord. For someone who doesn't know the living God, whatever common grace they know on this planet, it is but a moment, compared to an eternity in hell. If you want to know how really blessed you are, realize that you can have an entire lifetime of earthly suffering and the moment you see the face of God it will seem as nothing.

2 Corinthians 4:16 *So we do not lose heart. Though our outer self is wasting away, our inner self is being renewed day by day. [17] For this light momentary affliction is preparing for us an eternal weight of glory beyond all comparison, [18] as we look not to the things that are seen but to*

62

the things that are unseen. For the things that are seen are transient, but the things that are unseen are eternal.

GOD'S MERCIES RESULT IN JOY

If you look at the whole of your life and how the Lord deals with it, there are far more days of sunshine than rain. David describes this at the end of verse 5 in a very powerful way. He says, *Weeping may tarry for the night,* and the Hebrew word translated *tarry* can mean to lodge, to remain overnight in the sense of someone staying at a place. In the dark nights of our experience, weeping comes knocking at the door and lodges with us. But it's not for long, because in the morning a more permanent guest appears—joy. And, when he says *joy* comes, it's really a strong word, more than mild joy—the idea is a shouting kind of joy.

I love the fact that He doesn't present our hardships to us as though we're disobeying God by not being stoic. These things that we go through and test us, are hard. God doesn't call us to stoicism, and He doesn't chide us for hurting. There is weeping, but we must remember it's not forever, and that there's a good purpose for it, and that God has not abandoned us. Whatever weeping we know, it is only temporary, and shouts of joy are on the way.

2 Corinthians 4:16 *So we do not lose heart. Though our outer self is wasting away, our inner self is being renewed day by day. [17] For this light momentary affliction is preparing for us an eternal weight of glory beyond all comparison,"*

Do you believe that?

When Paul says it's *light*, it doesn't feel light, but compared with the blessings of eternity, it is both light and momentary. Compared with the glory that is going to be revealed, an eternal weight of glory, you can't even compare it. But the only way you can really see and believe and live in that is explained immediately in 2 Corinthians 4:18, *as we look not to the things that are seen but to the things that are unseen. For the things that are seen are transient* [here today, gone tomorrow, passing away], *but the things that are unseen are eternal.*

You need eternal vision to walk in these truths, and the only way to have eternal vision is salvation, which allows you to take hold of God's words and to know that they're true. So, you have a choice, don't you? Where are we going to set your focus? There are rainy days, but far more sunshine than rain. The question is, will you set your attention on the rain, or on the sunshine?

Alexander Maclaren made this point, "So it comes to be a piece of very homely, well-worn, and yet always needful, practical counsel to try not to magnify and prolong grief, nor to minimize and abbreviate gladness. We can make our lives, to our own thinking, very much what we will. We cannot directly regulate our emotions, but we can regulate them, because it is in our own power to determine which aspect of our life we shall by preference contemplate."[11]

You say, "I can't control how I feel." Oh, but you can! How? You must make a choice. Which aspect of your life will you prefer to contemplate, the weeping or the joy? The darkness or the light? The anger or the favor? The rain or the sunshine? And realize, even God's anger is loving. Even the sorrows are never wasted. There's a good purpose at

---

[11]Alexander Maclaren, *Expositions of Holy Scripture,* Accordance electronic ed. (Altamonte Springs: OakTree Software, 2006), paragraph 5669.

work in them. You have sorrows, but you also have great blessing. Where will you put your focus, what will be the part of your life that you really contemplate?

PERSONAL DETAILS
(30:6-10)

David has described his own situation in general terms, but now, in verses 6-10, he's going to give us an inside view. He moves from a more general description of God's deliverance of him to a more detailed description of it.

Psalm 30:6 *As for me, I said in my prosperity, "I shall never be moved." ⁷ By your favor, O LORD, you made my mountain stand strong; you hid your face; I was dismayed."*

Here he's describing a **painful discipline**. This is why earlier he speaks of the Lord's anger, and says, "It's just for a moment." He has met with the anger of the Lord and with the disciplining hand of his God. **He ties this experience to a time of pride in his life.**

There's debate about what exactly he has in mind, and there's no way to settle it. Some think the circumstances being described are those found in 2 Samuel 24 when David numbered the people and conducted that sinful census. The result was that the Lord sent a plague upon the people and tens of thousands died. Maybe during that time, David himself experienced this great sickness.

Whatever the specific circumstances, <u>David identifies his sin as that of self-confidence</u>. We see in verse 6, that during a prosperous time he said to himself, I shall never be moved. In verse 7, <u>David now sees that whatever strength he had was due to God's grace, God's *favor*, not due to anything that fueled his pride.</u> He came to this insight through the disciplining hand of God. Our pride will be exposed in every trial we experience, showing us our smallness, and drive us to acknowledge our need before God.

Do you do this? Do you give to yourself credit for the strengths that are only explained by God? Do you begin to feel strong, important and safe in yourself, and miss the fact that the only reason for these blessings of strength and safety is God's goodness to you?

At the end of verse 7 we see how the Lord awoke David to this realization. *You hid your face; I was dismayed.* <u>God made David feel what it was like without His favor, to be left alone in his own strength.</u> It was as though the clouds shut off the sunlight and he ran into a brick wall, afraid and troubled.

Now in verses 8-10, David tells us what he did in response. He cried out to God for mercy, the Lord's **powerful mercies**:

Psalm 30:8 *To you, O LORD, I cry, and to the Lord I plead for mercy". 9 "What profit is there in my death, if I go down to the pit? Will the dust praise you? Will it tell of your faithfulness? 10 Hear, O LORD, and be merciful to me! O LORD, be my helper!"*

The ESV translates verse 8 in the present tense, but most translations take the verbs in verse 8 to refer to the past: *To you, O LORD, I <u>cried</u>; to the Lord I <u>pleaded</u> for mercy.* That's probably the right way to understand it. He's telling us what happened at the time when it seemed the Lord had hidden His face, and what he did then, when he met with these circumstances that humbled him. Every hardship we go through is an opportunity to learn humility. God allows us to go through hard times. He allows us to feel our smallness and to know our mortality so that we recognize that He is

God, and we are not. He allows us to experience troubles so we might recognize that every good thing we experience is from His hand, not explained by us, but explained by Him. David had come to see that he needed God's grace, so he cried to the Lord. What was he crying for, pleading for? Mercy.

David's perspective changed as the Lord worked in his heart. **Not only is he seeking God's mercy, but he's seeking God's glory.** This is so important! Notice his motivation in verse 9: *What profit is there in my death, if I go down to the pit? Will the dust praise you? Will it tell of your faithfulness?* No longer is his desire for temporal deliverance, but for further opportunities to give praise and thanks to the glory of God. He will not forget where his deliverance and this mercy came from. David will give praise to God and tell of the Lord's faithfulness. This is why he's determined to do it in verse 1 and in verse 12. He's keeping his word.

Sometimes, we want deliverance, but we're not focused on God's glory. We want deliverance for our own sake, not for the sake of His name. But in verse 9, David wants the Lord's glory even while crying out to God for mercy. This is God's grace at work in his life. Only the Lord produces this kind of perspective. He is already anticipating what he wants to do in light of those mercies, and what he wants to do is to give glory to God. Is your desire for deliverance tied to your desire for God's glory?

So, David has sought God's mercy, God's glory and now, in verse 10, **he is seeking God's face.** David's cries are to God Himself. He isn't just asking for help; he is seeking God, his helper! *Hear, O LORD, and be merciful to me! O LORD, be my helper!"* He's focused not only on the hand of God or the help of God, but on <u>the face of God, the Lord as his helper.</u>

PROSPECTIVE THANKS
(30:11)

This psalm has been one of personal thanks and principled thanks, based on personal details of a painful discipline, followed by God's powerful mercies. Notice the outcome of all this.

Psalm 30:11 *You have turned for me my mourning into dancing; you have loosed my sackcloth and clothed me with gladness, that my glory may sing your praise and not be silent. O LORD my God, I will give thanks to you forever!*

David ends this Psalm with **prospective thanks, thanks not only for today, but forever**. He acknowledges that God is the One who explains him going from mourning to dancing, and from sackcloth to being clothed with gladness. God has fulfilled his desires to give Him glory, because here he is in the land of the living, and his voice will not be silent, vs. 12: *O LORD my God, I will give thanks to you forever.*

This is not just his story, but your story. The circumstances are different, but we walk with the <u>same God</u> and <u>experience the same kinds of mercies</u> every single day we live. And so, the question is, **do you give Him thanks?**

As Alexander Maclaren mentioned, which aspect of your life do you prefer to contemplate? Are you focused on the rain and forgetting the sunshine? Have you forgotten that even His disciplining hand is really the hand of a loving Father? **Do you have confidence that no matter how long the night seems to last, and no matter how real the weeping is, joy always comes in the morning for the child of God?** If you bear that in mind, you can rejoice even in the night, because the morning is on its way.

A Prayer During Times of Crisis

We have sinned against you so many times by not trusting you. You know our frame. You know that we're just dust. Sometimes, Lord, we do give in to the night, and we do give in to the weeping, and we forget that morning is coming. That never causes you to stop having pity upon us. Even then, Lord, you guide us through our tests and trials, and you see us through. Your hand sustains us. You incline your ear to us. You hear us. You hear our pleas for mercy. Work in our hearts, Lord, so that our greatest desire in all of our trials is your glory. Strengthen our hearts to be ready to give you praise and thanks for every good and perfect gift that comes down to us from you, the Father of lights, the God in whom there is no shadow or shifting. Your love is constant toward your children. Everything you've revealed about your character, we can stake our lives on. Every promise you've given is absolutely true. Strengthen us to see it and to say it, see it and to sing it until we see Jesus face to face. We pray for these things in Jesus' name. Amen.

Study Guide

The Cry from a Storm-Filled Heart: Psalm 43

1. What does James 1:2 tell us about our trials? Is that hard for you to remember when you're in the middle of a trial?

2. What is the connection between Psalm 42 and Psalm 43?

3. "Our God, in His sovereign and good plans, allows us to face situations that require us to persevere in thinking rightly." Do you think it's important to keep your thinking correct? If so, do you work at that? How?

4. What two things is the psalmist asking God for in verse 1?

5. Is the Lord the defender only of perfect people? What things do you see in this psalm that indicate the psalmist's ongoing relationship with the Lord?

6. How can the Lord's light and truth lead us to Him? And why is nearness to the Lord important?

7. Even in his troubled situation, the psalmist was committed to worship of the Lord. When your world is falling apart, do you tend to run toward the Lord and his church, or do you run away?

8. Have you ever tried singing praise to God when you felt horrible? (Remember also Paul and Silas in Acts 16:16-34.)

9. What kind of counsel or advice do you give to yourself? Where do you look for that advice—to political commentators? To self-help gurus and motivational experts? To tradition? Or to the Lord?

10. If you're going through a hard time right now, read verse 5 of Psalm 43 out loud to yourself.

After the Crisis: Psalm 56

1. Have you been in the habit of enjoying God? Or is that a new idea to you?
2. Without gossiping, do you recall times when you have been the victim of unfair attacks?
3. What is the basis of David's appeal for help?
4. When you're afraid, are you able to admit it and also to emphatically choose to trust in God?
5. Is it OK to ask the Lord to punish the wicked?
6. Do you believe the Lord really sees and cares about the wrongs you have suffered? If you do, how is that a comfort and encouragement?
7. Ponder the beginning of the quote from Charles Spurgeon, "The machinery of prayer is not always visible, but it is most efficient." Have you seen God's answers to prayer, either in your own life or in the lives of others?
8. How can trust in the Lord remove our fear?
9. While still in his crisis, David promised that he would someday worship and thank the Lord. Do any blessings come to mind that you've forgotten to thank Him for? Any promises that you made to Him while in crisis, that you have neglected to fulfill?
10. Is your goal to "walk before God in the light of life"?
11. Are you confident that the Lord's words are true? (They are.) Then preach them to your own soul.

Joy Comes in the Morning: Psalm 30

1. Have you ever been so sick that it seemed quite possible that you would soon die?
2. As James Montgomery Boice said, "Thanksgiving Psalms often arise out of lamentable circumstances." Do you recall times when the Lord has heard your

prayer and rescued you from sorrows hardships or dangers? Have you praised Him for those rescues?

3. What's the difference between being thankful, and being thankful to the Lord? Why is that difference important?

4. David encourages us to make his declaration our own. Have you considered praying Psalm 30 and other Psalms out loud (either speaking them or singing them) as a part of your worship?

5. If the Lord has rescued you from your guilt and from his wrath, have you thanked Him for it lately?

6. In what sense is the Lord's anger toward His own people momentary?

7. How can we know that there will be a "morning" with joy?

8. Do you usually think more about your sorrows, or your joys?

9. If you're in a very difficult situation right now, could it be

   a. Because you're being tested by the devil or his agents, as Job was in the Old Testament?

   b. Because of your own sin?

   c. Because of the Lord's loving discipline?

   d. Simply because you live in a broken world?

   e. Because of some combination of these things?

In each of these situations, what's the godly response?

10. In your troubles, when you pray, do you realize that you need the Lord's mercies? And are you concerned for His glory, or only for your relief?

11. When you are in a great difficulty, will you decide in advance that you will praise the Lord forever? How will this make a difference is the way you walk through the trial?

"The Psalms are a rich reservoir of truth, hope, and comfort for every believer. That's why I am thankful for my friend, Richard Caldwell, and his book *Hope for the Troubled Heart* wherein he exposits Psalms 43, 56, and 30. In this book, you will find careful exegesis from a seasoned ministry leader who brings these texts to bear in a hope-filled, pastoral way. I commend this little book for all who want to be uplifted by Scripture, and as a helpful resource to give to others who need the same."

Jason K. Allen, Ph.D.
President
Midwestern Baptist Theological Seminary & Spurgeon College

"I absolutely love this little book! It's yet another eminently practical guide from the pastoral heart of Richard Caldwell. With keen spiritual insight, Caldwell extracts the marrow from every line of the selected Psalms and skillfully ministers to the thoughts and intentions of the heart. I was greatly challenged and deeply comforted. It's the kind of devotional tool I will return to again and again, and one that will help all believers stir one another up to greater love for Christ and faithful obedience."

Pastor Jerry Wragg, D.Min.
Grace Immanuel Bible Church
Jupiter, Florida

"We can be certain that in this world we will have plenty of trouble. God, for his good purposes, will lead us through dark valleys that can be tremendously painful and even tempt us to lose heart. Thankfully, there is hope for the troubled heart—a kind of hope that gives life and calibrates our perspective. Richard Caldwell skillfully and faithfully unpacks and delivers this hope from three tremendously important psalms. If you are hurting or trying to minister to someone who is, the Psalms are what you need, and this book is a guide through those timeless lyrics, which will start to deliver hope today."

Pastor Mike Fabarez, D.Min.
Compass Bible Church
Aliso Viejo, CA